GALAXY STONE PAINTING

Project Book

Learn how to create a
collection of designs

5 projects inside

INTRODUCTION

Welcome to the wonderful world of galaxy stone painting!

This kit has been specifically designed for adults only.

Learning a new skill is always exciting – we're here to help you get started. Anyone can learn how to paint pebbles, and with so many designs, colours and sizes to choose from, the only limit is your imagination.
Let's get your creativity flowing and open your mind to this new and unlimited world. Pebble painting has become increasingly more popular over the years. You may even see them scattered around on your travels, especially around beaches and coasts.
You can create any designs and finishes – from positive affirmations to give as a gift, to a personal project as a calming pastime for yourself. The finished pebble can either have a matte or shiny finish.
This kit provides everything you need to make five painted pebbles. There are also four other projects, each with a step-by-step guide for you to try.
Remember, every skill takes effort to master, so don't be disheartened if it's not perfect the first time. The most important thing is that you have fun and enjoy yourself.
Ready to begin your pebble painting journey? Let's rock and roll.

KIT CONTENTS

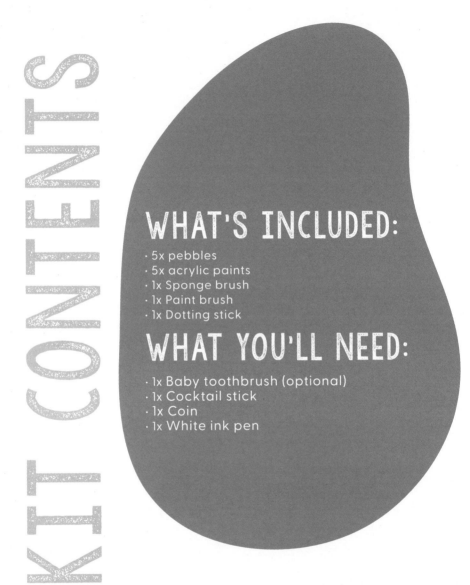

WHAT'S INCLUDED:

- 5x pebbles
- 5x acrylic paints
- 1x Sponge brush
- 1x Paint brush
- 1x Dotting stick

WHAT YOU'LL NEED:

- 1x Baby toothbrush (optional)
- 1x Cocktail stick
- 1x Coin
- 1x White ink pen

Ingredients:
Acrylic resin emulsion, Calcium carbonate, Glycerin, 2-Hydroxyethyl cellulose, Triethanolamine, Methyl 4-hydroxybenzoate, Hydroxyethyl cellulose, water. Pigment purple (permanent violet), White (Titanium dioxide) Blue (Ultra marine), Sky Blue (Phtalogyanine Blue).

PREPARING YOUR STONES

Make sure to wash your pebble with soap and water to remove any dust, (especially if you gather your own from the garden for the additional designs). Dry with a paper towel and let the pebble air dry completely. If you do collect any from the garden, check for any rougher patches and sand them down with sandpaper.

Some people prime their pebbles with a base coat of acrylic, but this is purely choice. Most people draw or paint directly onto them.

SEALING

To avoid your design getting ruined, seal your pebble with a spray sealer. If you want a glossy finish, you can use a varnish, sealer or a lacquer.

DESIGNS

In this booklet, we focus primarily on night sky designs, but this is not all you can do! Why not branch out and try some new themes? Broaden your creative horizons. Maybe dive into underwater scenes or get in touch with nature with a floral theme. Adding some gold leaf will create a dazzling and eye-catching geode! The world's your oyster! (Or pebble).

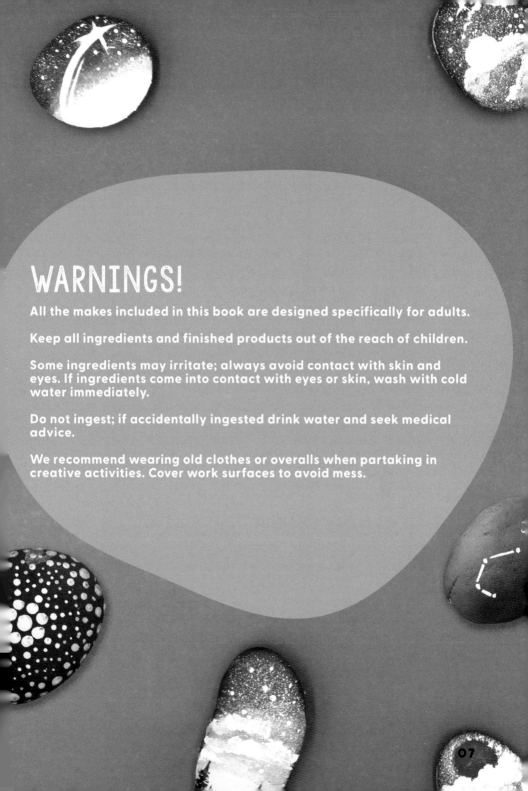

WARNINGS!

All the makes included in this book are designed specifically for adults.

Keep all ingredients and finished products out of the reach of children.

Some ingredients may irritate; always avoid contact with skin and eyes. If ingredients come into contact with eyes or skin, wash with cold water immediately.

Do not ingest; if accidentally ingested drink water and seek medical advice.

We recommend wearing old clothes or overalls when partaking in creative activities. Cover work surfaces to avoid mess.

TIPS & TECHNIQUES

Mixing paints - Try mixing the purples and blues to create more shades. This will help to create those beautiful gradients.

Dipping the sponge into the paint and dabbing downwards creates a faded effect and adds texture.

Wait for the first layer to dry before applying the second. You may find that the pebble absorbs the first layer. To avoid this, you could prep your pebble with a layer of acrylic paint.

If you don't want the hassle of prepping and sanding a natural pebble from your garden, you can buy bags of smooth pebbles from craft shops and online stores that stock them.

You don't have to use paints for pebble painting! You can use pens or paint pens as an alternative.

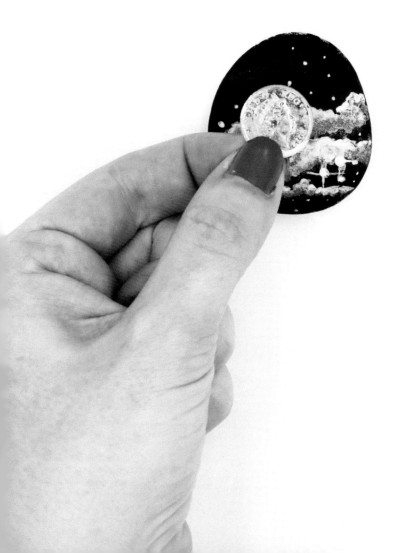

GALAXY STONES

GALAXY STONES

Create stunning designs with this step by step to guide to five Galaxy scenes. This contains everything you need. So, let's go!

YOU WILL NEED

- 1x Baby toothbrush (optional)
- 1x Cocktail stick
- 1x A coin
- 1x White ink pen

KIT CONTENTS

- 5x pebbles
- 5x acrylic paints
- 1x Sponge brush
- 1x Paint brush
- 1x Dotting stick

METHOD

FULL ECLIPSE

1. Empty your box of contents and place a single chosen pebble ready for painting on a clean, protected surface.

2. Once you've chosen your first pebble, use the deep galaxy blue paint for your background base. Using the brush, paint strokes up and down in both directions applying new paint each time. Make sure the edges are covered to obtain a more finished look.
Remember this step, as it will be repeated in the following designs.

TIP:
Allow the first layer to dry before applying a second layer - you may find that the pebble will absorb the first coat.

3. Once your pebble is dry, apply your next colour of choice. For this scene, the darker purple was used. Apply paint to the brush. Using the end of the brush, gently dab across the pebble to form your lowlight base layer for the clouds. Repeat the process in the lower half.

4. Using the lighter purple, apply the cloud highlight beneath the darker purple, then using the sponge tool, dab and blend downwards to create a faded effect.

TIP:
Try mixing the purples and blues to create different shades. The mixed shade will create more of a gradual, gradient of colour.

5. Once dry, get your white paint ready. Using a clean brush, start applying the white paint from the center of the pebble to form your clouds across the top half and the bottom half. Form the basic shapes, using less paint as the clouds move linear to the edge of the pebble. Use the sponge tool to fade the white paint downwards.

6. Once you're happy, using the tip of the brush, apply more white paint cautiously around the edges of the top half of the clouds to create more definition.

7. Add some stars! For the best results, use the stick supplied and dab the rounded end into the paint. Dot once or twice to create larger stars. With the fine end of the paint brush, gently stroke the paint outwards to form the star burst effect.

8. Dot white paint in areas to create slightly smaller stars where desired.

9. The eclipse. Once all clouds and stars are in place and aligned, it's time to locate your old tooth brush and coin – in this galaxy creation we used a 5 pence coin.
Place it where desired in the top half of the pebble. Once positioned, dip the toothbrush in the white paint. Using one hand, run your thumb slowly across the top of the brush, flicking paint across the pebble. Focus on and around the coin. Once dry, flip the coin off the pebble, revealing a neatly formed circle.

HALF MOON

1. Repeat step 2 with the pebble landscape, applying brush strokes diagonally across the pebble to create a more striped effect.

2. Repeat step 3 from pebble 1 using the darker purple to create the base layer. Mix the blue with white paint to create a mid-blue colour for the lowlights of the clouds above.

3. To form the clouds on this pebble, apply paint to the stick supplied and dot the rounded shapes of the clouds across the top half of the blue hues and the purple hues.

TIP:
Try dipping the sponge into the paint to form the lower areas of the clouds. Dab it downwards for a faded effect.

4. Dip the stick in white paint to dot in the star on the top right. Using the end edge, roll the stick outwards to form the starburst.

5. Repeat step 9 from pebble 1. Focus on flicking paint on the lower half of the pebble leaving a clearer night sky.

6. Once complete, add in the half moon. This can be tricky and will require some neatening of the edges for a crisper finish. To do this, use a white ink pen. Apply paint onto your brush using less pressure on the tip, then applying more pressure and more of the brush to flick around in a 'C' shape. Repeat this on top each time to thicken the moon.

7. Finally, use the paint brush to neaten the cloud edges for definition.

CLOUDY NIGHT SKY

1. Repeat step 1 with the pebble landscape, applying brush strokes diagonally across the pebble to create a more striped effect.

2. When your pebble is dry, apply your next colour of choice. For this scene, the darker purple was used. Apply paint to the brush. Using the end of the brush, gently dab across the pebble to form your lowlight base layer for the clouds. Repeat the process in the lower half.

3. When you have finished applying the base colour, let it dry. Repeat the same process with the painting of the clouds, feel free to mix up all the different methods to get thicker, fuller clouds.

4. Once dry, using the tip of the brush, apply more white paint cautiously around the edges of the top half of the clouds to create more definition. Try flicking paint from another paint brush to achieve larger splattered marks.

SHOOTING STAR

1. Repeat step 2 with the pebble landscape, applying the dark blue paint over the pebble.

2. Using each colour available, dab paint across the pebble, one colour after the other. Then with the sponge tool, blend each one into each other. Use darker colours first and lighter below.

3. Once dried, apply one larger circular star using the wooden stick and gently paint the stars shooting trail.

4. Flick some paint using your tooth brush across the top half (darker blue) area.

FULL MOON

1. Repeat step 2 with the pebble landscape, applying brush strokes diagonally across the pebble to create a more striped effect.

2. Repeat step 3 on pebble 1. Using the blue paint, fade the colour using the sponge brush in the top half. Apply the purple shade through the center, then add blue paint below in the second half.

3. Minimal clouds were applied on this design. Outline the blue and purple areas with a light white stroke and blend.

4. Flick some paint using your tooth brush across the top half (darker blue) area.

5. Once dried, apply the stars using the tip of your paint brush, dotting them around.

6. To paint the moon, dip your paintbrush into your white paint. In a circular motion, paint the moon mid-way on the pebble. Wait until this layer is dry before repeating again to achieve a solid white shape.

TIP:
Try using the sponge to create more of a texture across the moon.

NOTES

Use the space below to make your own personal notes on the previous project to help when you come back to make it again!

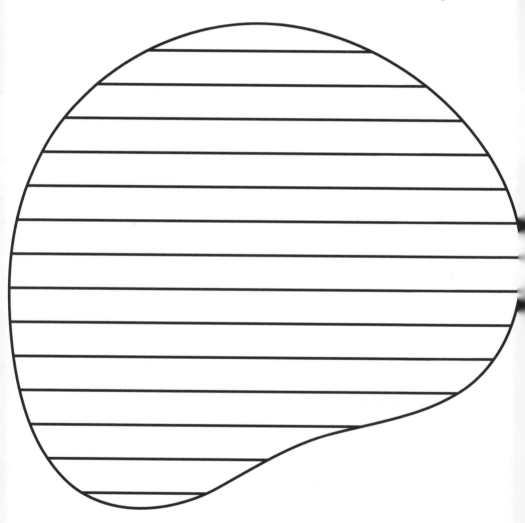

BOY ON
THE MOON

BOY ON THE MOON

Try these additional designs! 'Boy on the moon' is the first of a further four designs!

YOU WILL NEED

· 1x Large stone
· 1x Paintbrush
· 1x Cocktail stick
· 1x White ink pen/ white paint
· 1x Stencil

METHOD

1. Repeat step 2, from 'full eclipse', with the pebble landscape, applying the dark blue paint over the pebble with your paintbrush.

2. With your purple paint, create a circle in the center of the pebble. Using the white paint on top of the purple, continue to blend the paint adding more white paint as you move to then center of the pebble.

3. Once dried, add in some additional stars using a cocktail stick - this should give you a smaller dot. Allow to dry.

4. Once dry add a black circle of paint off centered on then pebble, allow to dry before applying the silhouette template (see next page).

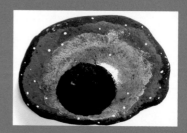

5. Cut the template provided to stick down onto the rock, (make sure the edges are fully stuck down with masking tape) alternativley stick the cut out onto the pebble when tacky.

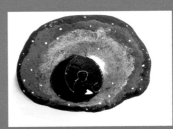

6. Once in place go over the template with a white paint to create the moon. Once partially dry you can remove the template to reveal the boy on the moon.

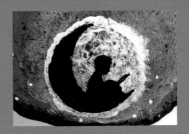

NOTES

Use the space below to make your own personal notes on the previous project to help when you come back to make it again!

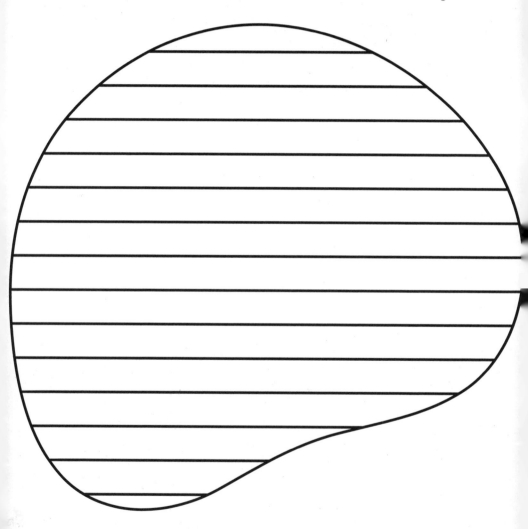

NORTHERN
LIGHTS

NORTHERN LIGHTS

Recreate one of the worlds most beautiful natural attractions, the Northern Lights!

YOU WILL NEED

- 1x Stone/Pebble
- 1x Paintbrush
- 1x Cocktail stick
- 1x Blue, 1x green and 1x white paint
- 1x Toothbrush
- 1x Black pen

METHOD

1. Repeat step 2 of the original make – (Full Eclipse) - and get your blue base layer onto a section of the pebble. Allow to dry.

2. Start using the same process and blend different gradients of colour downwards, dabbing the paint and layering. Use shades of blue mixed with white and a nice bright green to resemble the northern lights.

3. Once blended, add in some more strokes of paint using a lighter blue to give the sky- line some shape. Using the cloud process Step 5 in pebble 1- use blue paint and dab cloud shapes, so you create a duskier night sky.

4. Flicking paint - Using a toothbrush again, repeat the same process throughout the book, creating many individual stars. Fade the stars gradually downwards.

5. Add in silhouette trees with a black pen or a darker shade of blue. Finely draw the left and right branches in a triangular format, merging them into a center point. Make them taller at the outer edges and smaller as you come to the middle of the rock.

TIP:
Spray sealer or a sealant to protect and finish off the pebbles and to keep them preserved.

NOTES

Use the space below to make your own personal notes on the previous project to help when you come back to make it again!

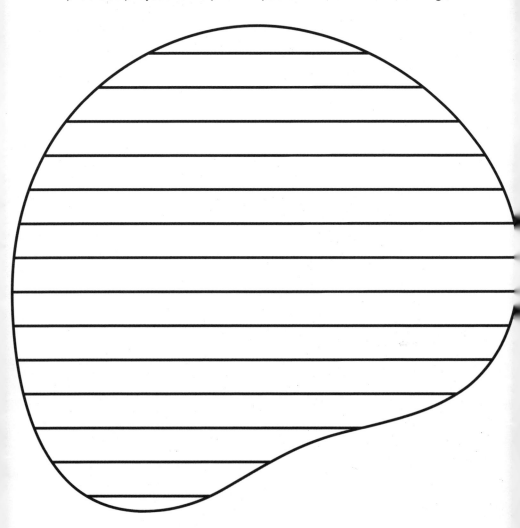

Libra

STAR SIGN

STAR SIGN

Set your star sign in stone with this cute and celestial design.

YOU WILL NEED

- 1x Stone/ pebble
- 1x Paintbrush
- 1x White pen
- 1x Blue, 2x Purple and
  1x Black acrylic paints

METHOD

1. Lay out the equipment you are going to use.

2. Start painting your rock blue. You will need more than one layer of paint for this to look its best.

3. Add two colours of paint, the lighter purple on the top half and the darker on the lower half, using the sponge tool, blend each colour into each other.

4. Add more paint in areas that require more, to define the base colour, keep using the dabbing effect until happy with your galaxy background.

5. Once happy allow the pebble to dry, in preparation for the next step, adding the constellation.

6. Once you have chosen your constellation, use white paint, or a white pen, to apply the first dot.

7. Apply each dot before joining the constellation. Once complete, use a fine paint brush to paint the lines to attach the dots.

8. Once all aligned, using the paint brush or pen, write the name of the star sign you've painted below. Allow to air-dry.

NOTES

Use the space below to make your own personal notes on the previous project to help when you come back to make it again!

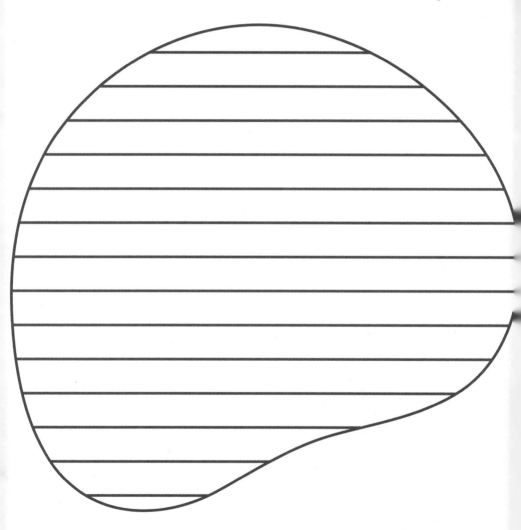

GOLD STAR BURST

GOLD STAR BURST

Creating this cute, bold design is simple and easy with very little equipment!

YOU WILL NEED

- 1x Stone/pebble
- 1x Black and 1x white acrylic paint
- 1x Paintbrush
- 1x Gold paint/pen

1. Lay out the equipment you are going to use. Start painting your rock black. You will need more than one layer of paint for this to look its best.

2. Wait until the paint has completely dried. Then using an end of a pencil or an item that can create a larger circle for the centre.

3. Apply your first white dot, gently push down and lift the item off the rock.

5. For the following dots use a cocktail stick,then gently apply further dots using the smaller end of the cocktail stick.

7. Apply the dots to the left and right side of the centrev dot.

8. Once done start applying the same process to each corner dot, dotting the circles diagonally outwards, to form a star burst formation.

9. Then using the cocktail stick fill in the gaps. Add 1-4 dots in between each section, so each dot proportionally fills the gap, making sure the dots get smaller as you work your way outwards. Apply these dots working your way around the pebble.

10. Once complete, use a gold pen or paint to fill in further gaps, but applying dots in the opposite process to the white dots.

Fill in gaps with smaller dots using the cocktail stick working your way outwards using larger dots, finishing with the larger dots around the edges of the pebble. These dots can be applied randomly but make sure you fill the gaps evenly.

Once dry, you can use spray sealer or a sealant to keep them preserved.

NOTES

Use the space below to make your own personal notes on the previous project to help when you come back to make it again!

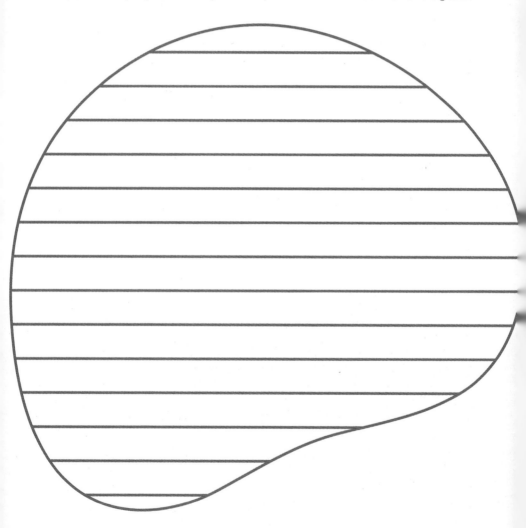